Letting in the Light

LETTING IN THE LIGHT

Poems by Kenneth Steven

First published in Great Britain in 2016

Society for Promoting Christian Knowledge
36 Causton Street
London SW1P 4ST
www.spck.org.uk

British Library Cataloguing-in-Publication Data
A catalogue record for this book is available from the British Library

ISBN 978–0–281–07670–3
eBook ISBN 978–0–281–07671–0

Typeset by Graphicraft Limited, Hong Kong
First printed in Great Britain by Ashford Colour Press
Subsequently digitally printed in Great Britain

eBook by Graphicraft Limited, Hong Kong

Produced on paper from sustainable forests

For Willow

It's when we are broken
We let in the light

———

Contents

Acknowledgements viii
Where 1
Early November 2
Sonnet in snow 3
Redbreast 4
The Strangers 5
Little Narnia 6
January 7
Listening 8
Understanding 9
The indefinable dark 10
Winter 11
Willow 12
Resurrection 13
Long ago 14
Living room 15
Daffodil 16
The ice 17
Father 18
Waiting 19
Sonia 20
Connemara 22

Whithorn 23
A different kind of light 24
Twelve 25
Stronvar 26
That August morning 27
Mull 28
August 29
Courbank 30
The forest 31
A turnip lantern 32
Ravens 34
Fetcham 35
In November 36
My child 37
Remembering 38
Alone 39
After winter 40
The ice 41
Understanding 42
Light 43
Let it be a garden 44
Christening 45

Acknowledgements

Poems in this collection have previously appeared in the pages of the following outlets: *Life and Work*, *Poetry New Zealand*, *Poetry Scotland*, *The Reader* and *Southlight*.

 WHERE

Nothing is sacred now
said the man who takes the five pounds
and seventy pence in the motorway service station
at ten thirty on a filthy Sunday night.
And I looked at the front of a lorry
hurtling out of the north with anger in its wheels,
its eyes grazing my face with their brightness
and I wondered. This used to be a place
for larks and meadow pipits and snipe
until we decided to bypass Sunderland –
now it's just the number of somewhere
we hammer north and south of.
And I drink sweet coffee and watch the windows
of the all night café
where the girl with the automatic smile,
the instant thank you, wipes away another customer
and smokes another cigarette.
I get out the map and lay it on the dashboard
and wish I could be back so much
it hurts the pit of my stomach –
and I realise, suddenly,
we spend the first eighteen years of our lives
desperately wanting away
and the rest of them trying to get home.

 # EARLY NOVEMBER

The morning the storm was gone
The fields thin with water
The branches waving bare,
Their last leaves curling the sky.

And there, in a land left gaunt,
Novembered by days of wild –
Swans, some folded against the wind
Some flying at half-mast above.

The huge slowness of their grace in the air
In the tangled wool of the sky;
Their beauty bigger in the buffeted air,
Their whiteness whiter.

They were ice carvings
Held and frozen high;
Hope of a new year still sleeping
In the land so sore below.

SONNET IN SNOW

How do you describe snow falling
Heavy from December sky?
There is no sound, there's less than sound;
The birds have gone as though they never were –
The trees wait with their arms outstretched
To fill with strangest shapes of snow.

And when you look across this world
Sky and fields and falling snow are all the same
And yet remain themselves,
Just as my steps across that world are there;
Every place I go remembered –
The journey of my life left,
Printed in a pressed shoe.

 REDBREAST

Eight below and I go out to give you crumbs
On the slab of wood that serves as a bird table.
I know you're a thug really; you chase the other birds away
And battle tooth and nail with all the other robins –
Yet I can't help marvelling at your startling orange breast
There on a winter's day, unafraid of the heavy thud of my
    boots.
You even come to my hand to eat, all however many grams
    of you –
There, trusting, in the very heart of my palm.
So, eight below on a dark December day
I still go out to give you crumbs, and wait for you to land
Soft as a moth, eyes bright chinks, your breast beating
Before nightfall swallows us all.

THE STRANGERS

When they arrived
everything was as it should have been:
the man was making something out of wood,
the girl slept. Sunlight danced with dust,
and the beasts shifted over on the side
that kept the shadow. The baby blinked in the light
and did not cry. The storm had passed
and everything had fallen back to normal.

Only then the unintelligible words
and inexplicable gifts; the strange simplicity
of the mystery. The echo that was left behind
when the door closed and the dark came back.

 LITTLE NARNIA

It was me who chose the name
and promised I'd put a lantern
up by the wicker gate where the wood begins.

I never did. How many thousand things
swept that promise away.

The wood and the wicker gate
they both remain, and the path through the wood
that leads to a point looking out to the hills
and the valley that lies in between.

Of all the promises I broke
that one makes me feel most guilty.

I look into the blackness deep
and midnight gives nothing back;
just the wet dark of December,
the window with the rain's crying.

I look out and think how once I imagined
holding your hand and going through the gate
into Narnia, and telling you stories
about dragons and magical journeys,
and how none of it now will happen –
the gate shut on that world for ever.

A place where it will always be winter
And Christmas can never come.

# JANUARY

Dark falls like a blanket. Flakes
Petal the wind in white scurries;
The road has gone soft and everyone is at home,
Watching the blue tanks of their televisions –
Peering out into the white silence of the snow.

We drive because we have to
And the car is a yellow cave.
We do not talk and quiet
Lies like a safe blanket between us.

The windscreen wipers flicker back white fudge.
Our world is fifty feet of road, two bright tunnels
Carved out of the nothingness of night.

I drift in and out of sleep, wanting to come home
And wanting to be set adrift in this huge journey,
For ever.

When at last we reach our reason for leaving
And climb out into silence
The stars have been born in a shingle of precious stones.

LISTENING

A sky from which all but the last blue has been lost
So the mountain against it stands like a great smoothed tusk
Wintered alone.

There is no wind, and yet
Sometimes the uppermost spindles of the birch trees dance
Criss-crossing the sky.

All of it about coming to a cabin to ask for quiet;
Waiting for blue lightning to flash the ground
Just once, and leave words burned in frozen snow.

 # UNDERSTANDING

coming home that night
rain slanting in against the windscreen
and suddenly I think of it like sadness
like a slow grief

January, the rain colder even than the snow
the sore lights of lorries stabbing past;
you driving and I useless in the other seat
polishing the words I never speak

wondering where we will be this time next year
not here, not in this place, surely
coming home and knowing deep inside
that home is where the hurt is

THE INDEFINABLE DARK

Three in the morning and I soft downstairs,
unable to find a way to sleep.

I sit at the edge of the table watching
beside an empty piece of paper.

There is no answer but the night:
God seems silent and the moon alone.

I am not brave: my smallness fills the room –
all I cannot find seems dark around me.

Sometimes when a poem's born it's like a jar
spilling to spread and fill the empty page.

The only way to conquer dark is being brave,
in listening for the dawn and waiting –

until the pen is filled once more,
and the poem takes its place in light at last.

 WINTER

I remember the feeling of leaving
to work some place down in England.

The train battled on, battled on, battled on
through the dreary sleet of the Midlands.

And I rejoiced in being homeless and lost
in the no man's land of the journey.

I stayed in a faceless hotel and was glad
of the lonely escape of the bedroom,

the breakfast with no one to talk to
the walk through the endless grey streets:

for all was the absence of war,
all was a leaving of fear –

and the only thing I dreaded, I know
was the coming back home in the end.

 WILLOW

We drove through the dark's fur
until the far glitter of Dundee.

The blue January night
like a cave, the city asleep.

I seemed to walk and walk and walk
the white miles of the hospital.

To a chamber that felt deep down –
dark and dreary and empty.

You smiled fear
from the contraption that held you open,

Lay waiting for the pain
to come and tear you again.

I said useless things
to try to comfort myself.

You shoved and there was nothing
but mess, the place's smell, the hours.

And then, at dawn, at last,
there slid into the world

This little girl, and I found myself crying,
that out of all the pain and blood should come

Such wonder.

 RESURRECTION

All winter the land lay for dead:
even lochs turned glazed eyes upwards,
pale and smooth their stares.

A whole month long the road snowed in:
nights a crackling of frost and stars –
waiting, watching, unsure and strange.

Only somewhere on the wandering road
at last, this morning, a flock of snowdrops
their white cries risen, their voices clear.

 LONG AGO

A house out of Jane Austen,
Among crows and ancient woods.

We went there sometimes to visit
A man who'd been a friend to my father.

I remember everything now except his name:
The frail hand that held my own too long,

The softly-polished words,
The water blue that made his eyes.

I stayed a while, not listening,
But hearing corridors and voices

Talking softly of time, of what would happen when,
Cutting it into lengths like silk.

I wanted out, into acres of emptiness,
Afternoons grey with ornamental walls and peacocks.

But the darkness of the place loomed over me,
Long before I learned what it was called.

All I knew was that I wanted home,
Where I had all the time in the world.

# LIVING ROOM

Now the storm of last night's passed;
everything lies torn in early morning

like a ship left tattered on the sea,
her rigging all in shreds, decks strewn with debris –

yet the storm itself forgotten, meaningless
beneath the glass-clear sky of morning.

You lie asleep, your hand curled white,
your breathing barely there at all;

and I come close on soundless feet and see
the shouting strewn about the floor,

the twisted arguments, the accusations –
I hear the echo of the long, slow crying

before the silence fell and we both crept away
to the corners of the dark, to gnaw the silence

and hear our hearts until we slept at last.
Now we have awakened into this strange day

and will not know what we should say or think
but look away, pretend, do everything

as if in some unwritten play, and acting badly –
wondering what happens next, how everything will end.

15

DAFFODIL

Out of the grey of winter
The hard of earth
A shriek of green
One single shoot
Spearing the sky.

Fighting upwards
Through February sleet
Waiting to change, to break
To the love of gold
The sunlight of spring.

 THE ICE

You were wrapped up like a caterpillar,
laid on a table and zipped into a green suit –
booted and gloved and ready.

The single blue pane of the skies;
the day holding its breath, the hills like crystals –
nothing but the sound of our steps.

I held you up to the sunlight
so the little circle of your face
turned gold and you closed your eyes.

I bent to hold the half of your hand
and stomp by stomp we went
to the puddle at the end of the road.

Like a blind eye it was
all frozen and fragments of ice;
carefully you crackled across.

And when we got to the other side
you turned and wanted back, and four times
we crunched slowly over.

How big small things can be.

 FATHER

It is the last picture of you:
standing half-turned away and smiling,
as though you are not ninety-one at all,
but twenty years your own junior
and ready to begin a walk
you'd planned for years and never done.

Is that where you went;
beyond the picture and into
the great landscape that you loved?
As though death was nothing more
than somewhere further than the camera could see;
made of the same moorland,
and full of birdsong that would never cease.

 WAITING

There are days when nothing happens:
the March sky wet with cloud, the cold
a raw ache grey in every room,
and through the window underneath the tree
the spines of daffodils clasped tight asleep.

The house is silent: the telephone
lies white across its cradle as though dead,
and from outside, far off, come voices without words.
There is no breath of wind: spring seems
still buried and impossible, so far away.

Sometimes then enough to know
blue sky will be again, and new buds
that break back into light. We wait like children,
patient, our chins on window sills –
watching and believing – a little longer yet.

 SONIA

Why the angel came she never knew.
She'd found the feathers some time back against the wall;
A little circle of them, white as snow, and soft to touch.
She'd thought it was a bird, a collared dove.

He told her there were more things than she would ever know
Beneath the skies; more things she could ever guess were
    good.
She listened, heart on fire, behind the house –
There in a town that had been asleep since 1952.

Her marriage dead and buried twenty years;
They had said all there was to be said
And lived on in the same house silent
Speaking only answers.

The television babbled about films and holidays and
    laughter,
Stood empty only in blue darkness when she came down
At three each morning, sleepless, to make a cup of tea.
She sat listening to the fingertips of rain

Wondering what her son was doing out in Amsterdam,
Thinking about what might have happened if –
As though there was some secret door that she could find
To slip out still and grasp the offered hand.

It was when she took the rubbish out she met the angel.
She stood in brightness and it was like
A glade of light she'd found when she was five years old.
Everything else was gone; he held her with his eyes.

She didn't tell a soul. Who would believe she'd met an angel
On a Saturday in March behind the house?
She kept him, like a flower in a book, pressed clear and
    whole:
The light alive inside her, dancing ever more.

# CONNEMARA

From out of greyness and the months of storm –
wonderful landings of stories, shipwrecks of things,
to be handed down from mother to son,
their frayed edges mended, and sometimes new pieces
woven in from moor and mire.

All are kept safe in the drawers of everyday,
between the stone floor and the low roof,
then brought out when least expected:
lights on moorland, songs of blind harpers,
journeys to the other world, caves of gold,
stories of those with the gift of the second sight.

And then the ordinary again,
the bringing in of turf for the fire,
in among and tucked beside
the everything else that always must be done.

 WHITHORN

suddenly the light blows back
seams of gold, little flickers
in the tattered yellow dresses of daffodils
in this south-west corner, this first day of spring

here in the kite upwards whirl of the wind:
crows like flakes of ash playing and croaking,
the blue skies big, blown about and battered;
the dented hills mauve, hunkered down among the clouds

and coming home I saw Vincent in a field
dragging his canvas into the light,
exulting the wind
his bracken head bright, happy and mad

A DIFFERENT KIND
OF LIGHT

To climb out of the known
into the moorland's empty miles;
where sun and shadow meet
and the only elements the ones
that first began this world:
wind and water, rock and light.

You crouch beside the loch,
out of the bullying of the breeze –
and nothing might have changed
since the beginning;
a smear of brightness smiles the water,
before going back to grey.

Somewhere unseen the sadness of a bird –
a single song in the hugeness of the sky,
and suddenly you know you do not matter
here beyond the normal and the everyday,
the old enslavement of the hours –

you have escaped to breathe
a different kind of light.

 TWELVE

The way once upon a time it was:
when nights lay empty of their birdsong,
and the sun all swollen red went down,
and you among the boys went running,
a whole hill upwards into dusk –
where the badger setts lay shadowed,
and stillness danced with midges all around.

Then you knew there might be magic –
perhaps a falling star, or fox cubs,
or the finding of a cave that no one else had seen.
Most of all it was the thrill of this;
the being twelve years old and knowing sure
that all the summer lay ahead and many more,
that it was yours like wild fruit heavy, ready –

in the fields and fields and fields far out of sight.

STRONVAR

He is lifted out of the town
To the month of June. A wooden house
Whose bare feet have grains of sand.
That night a blue sky, deep and so
It would be possible to walk for miles.
Every without fail he wanders
Underneath the torn shreds of gulls –
Laps his toes in the cold see-throughness,
Plays in starfish pools of light.
He comes back and lays out stories
Talks them all with open hands.
They smile him, carry him
To watch a whole moon, orange
Globe slow and shuddering above the night.
But when they tell him that tomorrow
Will be going home, his eyes laden
And he rocks and breaks their night,
His skin still salty when he sleeps.
He carries all the fragments of those days,
Careful, fragile, always.

THAT AUGUST MORNING

I remember a summer
the days hung yellow and would not move,
and I leaned out at night to thick, warm darkness –
the air all made of moths, the trees held breathless.

And when the thunder came at last I loved the fear of it;
the flickering that lit the hills, the seconds held,
before the grumbling and the boom of anger –
the hissing singing of the rain.

I remember that morning after storm:
I crept the stairs, went out to stand in sun,
beneath the shadow play of swifts –
the whole sky blue, the air left deep and clear.

And whether you believe in God or not,
I did that day, still looking up, eyes closed –
my life in purest light.

 MULL

That moment you round the corner
I love the most. Ben More stretched out west;
headlands and a scattering of islands,
wind tugging at the guy-ropes of the sky,
to turn it all from brilliance into gloom.

Down and further out among a rubbled shore of boulders,
salt marsh born for otters, a hundred places made for hiding;
and if you walk there, circled by the calls of redshank,
you are only small, so hunched and useless
in the greatness of the wind, just trying to keep your feet.

Further on, out towards Iona, stunted oaks and rowans,
places where the rivers fall in shining to the sea.
All of it a worthless place: broken, tangled, lost –
yet every time I make the journey back it's here I break,
am filled brimful with light another time.

 AUGUST

A small plane hummed the sky at noon;
went missing, presumed dead, in the clouds.

When it grew dark, purple bruises
hid among shrubs and damaged the trees.

A moon tried to climb from the west,
then broke, spilled quicksilver over silent fields.

A salamander's tongue. Three miles later
the thunder answered like a rousing bear.

The rain. The pure soft song of rain
silking the whole world, healing the fever.

 COURBANK

I stand in the centre of the garden
smelling the wetness after rain;
the globes of raindrops in the roses
as up above, in cleared sky
the promises of blue beyond the grey.

The swallows flicker, swivel still;
they make no sound, their dark shapes
vanish and then come back.
Half an hour ago there was a thatch of birdsong –
now it's just the few last notes, so rich and slow.

Why should the heart hurt now, on such a night;
why here in this long globe of light
in June, the very midpoint of the year?

Perhaps I want for ever all this loveliness
and know deep down I hold it but a blink.

 THE FOREST

Let there be days
you are no longer all the things you have to be
but just the child inside, waiting
there at the edge of the forest.

You walk, as though into your own first book of stories,
and behind you the dark closes like a door.
You stand, small, in a woollen blanket of silence
that is not silence at all.

Somewhere the soft movement of water
the dust dancing in a scattering of light;
more unknown than ever will be known,
and the thrill of that beginning in your heart.

Make no mistake: this is once upon a time –
you are a story waiting to be told.

 A TURNIP LANTERN

You'll bounce up and down beside me
as I put the turnip on the table –

the table that comes up
no taller than your tummy.

I'll kneel, start scooping out
a soft mash of turnip,

and as I dig and spoon
I'll tell you of the Halloweens

Nic and I went out with lanterns,
dressed as ghosts or pirates,

swaying our turnip lanterns,
their eerie orange glows,

knocking on the doors we dared:
singing songs, reciting verse –

then opening our bags
for a cascade of coins and fruit.

Now in the turnip lantern
I'll cut a mouth and eyes

you'll bounce the more beside me,
your eyes all shining bright

and then I'll bury a candle
deep in the very heart –

I'll spark a match and light it
and gently fix the lid;

we'll go into the garden,
the grey October dusk

and I'll put the lantern's string
in the small pride of your hand.

 RAVENS

I heard them
like living pieces of coal in the thrown-back sky;
I heard them and could not see them –
searched uselessly the grey being tugged like a kite,
the rain thrashing the road.

There, and there –
bedraggled rags of black,
playing with the wind, folding and unfolding;
and I thought of the ravens the travellers kept,
clever enough to climb through a bedroom window
for glints of rings and gold –
wise birds that might have carried word once
of battles and royal births.

And I saw myself
staring into the fun and games of their sky,
small on a November morning.

FETCHAM

November 5th and the whole night huge;
I woke and a fox's voice was rasping
over the gardens and the sculpted woods,
at two in the morning and the world asleep.

That night the skies had bloomed with fireworks;
burst and fluttered till they fell back dark.
The parties over and the lights put out,
the doors all clicked and the streets left still.

When I woke up the night was full,
a silver brilliance with the moon's ship high;
the great sky shining and the stars red fires,
and the rasp and the rasp of a fox's bark.

IN NOVEMBER

I think of them as First World War days
When the mist is thick as smoke;
The woods and hills all swallowed, gone,
And a cold rawness hanging in the air.
I thud out sometimes to the edges of the trees;
Imagine my father coming towards me out of silence,
As though nothing at all had changed, as though death
Had never happened, as though the years between
Were rubbed away. And in those days
There is no breath of wind, the land lies still,
The river greys into the empty distance,
Carrying the fallen colours of the woods, and leaving us
Alone and strange in the year's last dark –
Waiting and watching, for what we do not know.

MY CHILD

I dreamed I went out to look for you
one night, knowing that you were lost.
No stars, just darkness, and still the rain.
I carried a torch that leapt and breathed, a living flame
and went out into the fields, calling your name;
I wandered through water the whole night through
and still I did not find you, and came back broken –
tired and hungry, hopeless. But still I knew
that you were there, somewhere in all that dark,
and I left the outside light shining
that you might always find the way back home.

 REMEMBERING

Almost Advent and the day with blue panes in grey sky.
It's rained so long no one remembers when it started;
the valley left a World War One-scape, its Paul Nash trees
hung dark and breathless. Through it all a river,
swollen like the scaled thickness of a snake, shining out
on that slow eternal coiling to the sea.

I sit in the cabin writing, listening and not listening
to small pieces of birdsong; the jewellery of little birds
scattering across the morning somewhere up above.
And then, far off, I hear their ragged voices;
let the pen fall, thinking of my father, as if
he'd always told me to be ready, to keep listening,
to give up whatever else that I was doing to find them –
to stand and watch, look up, as once he taught me.

I struggle to my feet, knocking back the chair;
don't stop to pick it up, for now they're overhead –
swimming in three skeins, already passing, heading
on into the panes of blue. *Geese.*
And I think of him and stand there still, his boy,
looking up, remembering.

 ALONE

That Christmas I camped in the house
surrounded by a marriage in boxes.

And the house smelled damp
as though grief had seeped in the walls;

I did not want to be there
in the eerie silence of the place –

the house singing at night,
a constant chiming of droplets.

It rained when it should have snowed
till the December fields were afloat

and farms shone out in the darkness
like silent cries for help.

I lit the fire, crouched in front of its glare
saw the ghosts that danced in the flames.

AFTER WINTER

Sometimes we cannot see the stars
The dark is down and holds us bleak and lost
Sometimes all that we can do is wait
For believing's just too big and too alone.

Until a snowdrop pushes up the sky
And suddenly the snow is only slush
The winter no more than a waiting for the sound
Of geese in thousands overhead.

THE ICE

One pure blue January day
I fought the hillside to find the loch –
a whole white eye of winter,
a lid across its lapping;
a held breath that kept the water clenched.

No sound, just light fiercing the silence,
and nothing for a hundred miles.

I dared to brave the ice
to place my weight beyond.
Like Christ I walked on water, step by step
out to the very middle of the loch;
something that could not be, that was impossible –
a miracle that was only mine.

 # UNDERSTANDING

Sometimes it is all right not to be afraid;
to forget, to open wide the windows on the night
and lean out, listening, to the stars.

Sometimes it is not wrong to just rejoice
in the slow river in its blue road slipping east,
as dark comes down at midnight after day.

Sometimes it is safe to be at peace with this,
to leave what we have carried all the years
and take our shoes off for the softness of the grass.

 LIGHT

Sometimes it's not about delays and cancellations;
the door that needs repaired, the shopping left behind.
You come home early and find yourself alone:
the sun blooms pink against the kitchen window,
and there's the whisper of a butterfly against the glass.

You slip inside a place where hurry doesn't happen,
and stand there, listening,
as raindrops glisten all the way along the sill.

You scrape a chair back, sit down softly
as though you were in church, your hand across the table.
For in your mind you're back in childhood –
the film of it is faded in your eyes and yet it's there.

And everything you have to do and have to be
seems suddenly to matter less than what the robin sings
this April evening as the sun comes glinting here and there
about the house. For all these little things
are fragments of the light that make up life.

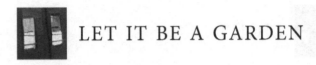# LET IT BE A GARDEN

unopened into light
the rose gathering her warmth
to sun the silence and to still
this step we bring inside –
our loudness and our doubt;
to down the noise of all our talk
and be inside a quiet for a time,
to learn what quiet means and heals –
to take it back at last outside
and break small pieces for the ones
who have not heard or held
what gift was ours

CHRISTENING

We drove through grey silence;
the skies drifting with snow
in a winter that would not end.

At the church I made promises
in a language I did not know –
and a German bell rang out,
strange in the muffled day.

And then you ran to me, Willow,
and you carried the sun in your running;
you poured into laughter and ran
as though all the war was over.

And inside a shell broke
that Easter Sunday morning;
a shell like a bird's egg
flooded over with warm light.

The long folly of words,
the gunneries of rage,
the anger of small conflicts –
useless, forgotten, gone.

The land left open
for the love of sunlight –
the beginning of another spring.

Did you know that SPCK is a registered charity?

As well as publishing great books by leading Christian authors, we also . . .

. . . make assemblies meaningful and fun for over a million children by running www.assemblies.org.uk, a popular website that provides free assembly scripts for teachers. For many children, school assembly is the only contact they have with Christian faith and culture, and the only time in their week for spiritual reflection.

. . . help prisoners to become confident readers with our easy-to-read stories. Poor literacy is a huge barrier to rehabilitation. Prisoners identify with the believable heroes of our gritty fiction. At the same time, questions at the end of each chapter help them to examine their choices from a moral perspective and to build their reading confidence.

. . . support student ministers overseas in their training through partnerships in the Global South.

Please support these great schemes: visit www.spck.org.uk/support-us to find out more.